STOICISM FOR

BEGINNERS

Master the Art of Happiness. Learn
Modern, Practical Stoicism to Create
Your Own Daily Stoic Routine.

Kevin Garnett

ERRORS

Please contact me if you find any errors.

My publisher and I have taken every effort to ensure the quality and correctness of this book. However, after going over the book draft time and again, we sometimes don't see the forest for the trees anymore.

If you notice any errors, I would really appreciate it if you could contact me directly before taking any other action. This allows me to quickly fix it.

Errors: errors@semsoli.com

REVIEWS

Reviews and feedback help improve this book and the author.

If you enjoy this book, I would greatly appreciate it if you were able to take a few moments to share your opinion and post a review online.

Table of Contents

Introduction

It's quite extraordinary that the teachings of a former slave, the diary of a great Roman emperor and the personal letters of a great Roman playwright survived.

What's even more remarkable is the wisdom they all convey: Practical advice on how to live your life.

Advice that is as true in today's demanding society, as it was thousands of years ago!

Are you:

- struggling with anger, fear and anxiety?
- looking for a way to improve the quality of your life and make happiness a permanent part of your life?

By applying the principles of Stoicism, you can achieve all this!

For over two thousand years, scholars, aristocrats and the general public have been enchanted by Stoicism, which is one of the longest persevering Western philosophical schools. Millions of people around the world have used the principles of Stoicism to improve the quality of their lives and to eliminate negative emotions such as anxiety, fear, anger and dissatisfaction from their lives.

The power of Stoicism lies in the fact that it engages the whole range of human experience. It addresses different topics like emotion, rationality, will and piety.

Stoicism is an *active* philosophy. This means that simply knowing its principles and doctrines is not enough. Stoicism requires that you:

- live your life according to these doctrines and,

- develop habits that help you practice its principles.

Therefore, this book will be very practical. Apart from simply teaching you about the principles of Stoicism, it will also provide you with action steps that you can follow to implement Stoicism in your life.

Are you ready to turn your life around? Let's dive in!

Chapter One: What Is Stoicism

In this chapter, you are going to learn what Stoicism is and where it originates.

In recent years, interest in the ancient philosophy of Stoicism has experienced a renaissance. Despite the growing popularity of this older philosophy, there are still so many misconceptions about it. For instance, many people believe that Stoicism is about being devoid of any emotion, including happiness. Others think that to be a stoic, you need to lead a Spartan and bland lifestyle. To set the records straight, let's take a look at what Stoicism really is.

What is Stoicism?

Stoicism is a philosophy that helps us maintain control over our thoughts and actions in a world full of chaos and unpredictability. Stoicism understands that we have no control over external occurrences, and therefore we should not rely on them. Instead, we should rely on our mind, behavior, and reaction to external events, all of which we can control. Stoicism teaches us that what matters is not what *happens* to us, but rather, how we *react* to it. In a world of chaos, Stoicism teaches us how to remain steadfast, strong and in control of ourselves.

Most of our dissatisfaction in life occurs because, rather than using logic, we have an impulsive dependency on our reflexes. Stoicism helps us to:

- overcome these destructive emotions,
- act on what we can act upon, and
- accept things that we cannot act upon.

Rather than being a philosophy of endless debate, Stoicism is **focused on action**.

The core principle of this ancient philosophy is that we need to overcome our insatiability in order for us to lead good and meaningful lives. Most people today live their lives like slaves, always in pursuit of happiness. Every person has a long list of desires that they are trying to satisfy. Even those you consider to have attained success have more things they want to achieve. The problem is that, once one desire is satisfied, it tends to be immediately replaced by a new one. This keeps most of us in continuous chase, always trying to satisfy our desires. After a lifetime of pursuit, we are no more satisfied than we were at the very start. This way, we end up wasting our lives instead of living for each moment.

Stoicism is a philosophy that should be applied in our day to day lives. It focuses on ethics (how we live our lives), which are in turn influenced by the natural world and logic. The resurgence of the popularity of Stoicism in the modern world has been driven by the fact that the philosophy aims to teach us how to attain peace, joy and tranquility in the midst of struggles and hardship.

The Origin of Stoicism

Stoicism was founded in Athens in the early 3rd century BC. The philosophy was founded by a Phoenician merchant and philosopher known as Zeno. Zeno was born in Citium, a town in Cyprus, and lived from 334 to 262 BC. At around the age of 34, during one of his travels, Zeno was shipwrecked. Luckily, he survived and found himself in Athens. Having lost everything and with nothing else to do in life, he visited a bookseller in Athens. It is here that he found a book that would lead him on the path of becoming a philosopher. After learning under Crates of Thebes and the philosophers of the Megarian School, he then began teaching and practicing his own philosophy. His school of philosophy was known as Zenoism, before the name was later changed to Stoicism. The name Stoicism was derived from the Stoa Poikile, a 'painted porch' from where Zeno used to give his lectures. His students became known as 'Stoics'.

Stoicism was not a philosophy that was reserved for the aristocrats. It was a philosophy of the street, open for ordinary people. A *working class* philosophy, if you will! Anyone could go to the Stoa Poikile and listen to the teachings of Zeno.

The philosophy taught and practiced by Zeno as well as other Stoic philosophers was heavily influenced by the works of Socrates. Apart from Socrates, Stoicism was also influenced by the Cynics, the Skeptics and the Academics (the followers of Plato).

While Stoicism was founded by Zeno, one of the most influential Greek Stoics was Chrysippus, who was one of Zeno's followers. Chrysippus is said to have elaborated most of the doctrines that are associated with the philosophy to this day. Apart from Plato, Socrates and Aristotle, Chrysippus is believed to be the greatest ancient philosopher. Though he is believed to have authored over 700 works, unfortunately none of them survived.

Despite having originated in ancient Greece, the greatest influence of Stoicism would be felt centuries later when it got to the Roman Empire. Most of what is known about Stoicism today comes from the ideas and writings of the Roman Stoics. Some of the most influential Stoics from this era include Epictetus, Musonius Rufus, Seneca and Marcus Aurelius.

Owing to the kind of lives led by the early Stoic philosophers, Stoicism was perceived as a very practical and very useful school of thought from its early stages. It later moved from Athens to the West, where it gained lots of popularity. However, the adoption of Christianity as the official Roman religion and its subsequent spread to the west led to the decline of Stoicism and several other ancient Greek philosophies. People abandoned this ancient philosophy to the point where it almost became extinct.

Fortunately, Stoic Philosophy started making a comeback in the late 20th Century. This resurgence has been driven by a number of factors. These include the adoption of the philosophy by celebrities and pop culture idols, featuring of the philosophy in the works of renowned authors as well as the growing interest in self-development. Some popular business and political leaders who have been known to practice Stoicism include Bill Gates, Warren Buffet, Tim Ferris, Tony Robbins, Presidents George Washington and Theodore Roosevelt, as well as actor/musician LL Cool J.

In the next chapter, you are going to learn the key beliefs and principles beliefs of Stoicism.

Chapter Two: The Key Beliefs and Principles of Stoicism

In this chapter, you are going to learn the beliefs and principles that form the foundation of the philosophy of Stoicism.

They are based on the teachings of three Stoic leaders:

- **Marcus Aurelius**: Aurelius was an Emperor of the Roman Empire, and the last one among the five so-called good Emperors. Perhaps you remember him from the first scenes of the 2000 movie *Gladiator*. During this time, Aurelius was the most powerful person on earth. He had everything under his command, he could fulfill any of his desires, yet he exercised great restraint against his temptations. Each evening, Marcus

Aurelius sat down alone, reflected on his day and wrote his thoughts in a private diary. His diary was later published as the book *Meditations*. This book has been one of the most significant sources of knowledge about Stoic philosophy.

- **Epictetus**: Despite the fame he had attained by the time of his death, Epictetus was born as a slave. Epictetus discovered Stoicism through another Stoic philosopher known as Musonius Rufus. When he gained his freedom, Epictetus founded his own school and went ahead to teach many great people in Rome, one of whom was Marcus Aurelius. Epictetus never wrote down his teachings. His influence came by pure luck through one of his students – Arrian – who wrote down his teachings. Arrian wrote two books, Discourses and Enchiridion, which contain most of the teachings of Epictetus.

- **Seneca**: Seneca was a renowned playwright, an advisor to emperor Nero, and one of the wealthiest people within the Roman Empire. Seneca was exposed to Stoicism by Attalus, a Stoic philosopher who tutored him in his early life. He was also a great admirer of Cato. Many of Seneca's personal letters and writings survived after his death and have been a great source of knowledge on Stoicism. Seneca's writings had great influence on some notable people, including Erasmus, Pascal, Francis Bacon and Montaigne.

With that out of the way, let's dive into the most important beliefs and principles of Stoic philosophy.

Acknowledge That Some Things Are Out Of Your Control

Stoic philosophy requires us to understand that there are things within our control and those that we cannot control. If something makes you unhappy and it is within your control, then you should do what you can to change it. However, if it is not within your control, it makes no sense getting worked up over it since there's nothing you can do to change it. This principle helps us to live a life of satisfaction and confidence.

For instance, if you are going to a job interview, your preparation for the interview is within your control. You should do everything within your ability to ensure that you are well prepared. However, you have no control over the outcome of the interview. Therefore, you should not beat yourself up if you fail to qualify. Instead, you should let it go since you know you played your part to the best of your ability.

Acknowledge That You Are The Source Of All Emotions

"Today I escaped anxiety. Or no, I discarded it, because it was within me, in my own perceptions. Not outside." - Marcus Aurelius

As a student of Stoic philosophy, one thing that you should understand is that all the emotions we experience are not a result of some external events. Instead, these emotions are a direct result of how we choose to react to these events.

For instance, if you are late for a meeting, it isn't the fact that you are late that is stressing you out. Instead, your stress comes from your thoughts about what will happen *as a result of* not being on time. Instead of allowing this to stress you, you should realize that it has already happened and that there is nothing you can do about it. From there, you can remain calm and think of ways of handling the situation without getting worked up.

This is something that is very common in our lives. When we have bad emotions, the easiest thing for us to do is to place the blame on outside forces. This makes us feel good about ourselves and keeps us from taking responsibility for our emotions. However, what we forget is that by doing so, we are merely deluding ourselves. Therefore, any time you experience bad emotions, don't be quick to find the external cause of your turmoil. Instead, acknowledge that these emotions come from within. By acknowledging this, only then can you change the emotion to a positive one.

Live Every Day Like Your Last

Steve Jobs once said that the best thing that ever happened to him was to have a close encounter with death. It made everything else irrelevant and gave him a clear view of what he wanted out of his life. Similarly, many great people will tell you that they were spurred by near-death experiences. Stoic philosophy understands this and encourages us to live *every day* like our last.

When you approach life with the attitude that you will live forever, you get a false sense of belief that you have time to accomplish everything you want. You tend to procrastinate on things and waste your time on useless things.

However, once you realize that your time on earth is limited, all useless things fade away. You stop living your life to please others. You have no fear of embarrassment. Instead, you start living life on your own terms. You are not afraid of trying new things if you know that this is the only time you have. This is why Stoicism encourages its followers to meditate about their death. Once you understand that the world will continue spinning even after you are gone, it will spur you to make the most of the time you have.

This principle is captured perfectly in the words of Seneca:

"You live as if you were destined to live forever, no thought of your frailty ever enters your head, of how much time has already gone by you take no heed. You squander time as if you drew from a full and abundant supply, though all the while that day which you bestow on some person or thing is perhaps your last."

Don't Fear Failure, Fear Regret

How many times does the fear of failure keep us from going after the things we want? The fear of getting rejected keeps us from going after that person we like. The fear of looking dumb keeps us from sharing our ideas, even if they would have provided the perfect solution. Fear keeps us from going to the interview for that job we covet.

Stoic philosophy teaches us that we should not be afraid of failure. This is because the things we are afraid of trying are the things that would actually lead to growth for us. We should accept failure as a part of life and learn to embrace it as a source of learning. The only person who has never failed is he who has never tried something new. Failure is not the end of the world. According to Stoic philosophy, it is better to try and fail at something than to live with the regret of what we could have achieved if only we had tried.

Stoicism encourages us to practice misfortune, to meditate about bad things. This prepares us in advance and teaches our minds how to react in such situations. By meditating about things going wrong, we realize that we can still survive even after they happen. The best way of eliminating fear is to look at things practically and see that you can handle the worst-case scenario. When you know that failure is not the end of life, you will be able to keep trying even after encountering failure. Facing and overcoming failure also molds and strengthens our character.

Practice Awareness

Another important principle of Stoicism is mindfulness. We need to be self-aware and mindful of our actions. Awareness means that we should always be present, instead of running on autopilot mode. Before taking any action, we should think through its repercussions. Without doing this, it becomes impossible for us to act rationally.

To practice awareness, try focusing on the present moment. Clear your mind of thoughts of what you need to do later or what you should have done before. Focus your thoughts on where you are and what you are doing. If you are walking, feel your feet connect with the ground as you take each step. If you are just seated, try to focus on your breathing. When you find yourself experiencing a new emotion, acknowledge the emotion by telling yourself what you are actually feeling. Only by acknowledging the feeling can you determine the best way to respond to it. If you don't know the emotions that are driving your actions, it becomes very difficult to change your behavior.

In today's chaotic world, it is not always possible to remain present. Sometimes, emotions will dictate your actions even without your knowledge. To remain aware, you should make a habit of going through your day each evening. This allows you to identify instances where you acted out of emotion. You can then deliberately decide how you will react when faced with a similar situation.

If you are always preoccupied with thoughts of the past or future, you are actually not living your life to the fullest. Remember, the past and future do not exist. The only thing that *really* exists is the present, which is what you should always strive to make the most of. This is best expressed by the following quote:

"But life is very short and anxious for those who forget the past, neglect the present, and fear the future. When they come to the end of it, the poor wretches realize too late that for all this time they have been preoccupied in doing nothing." - Seneca

When you do things without awareness, without being present, you leave yourself to be guided by your instincts, which are often controlled by your emotions. It is easier to make irrational decisions when we let instincts guide our actions. To avoid this, always focus 100% on whatever you are doing at that particular moment in time.

The Greatest Virtue Is to Live A Rational Life

This principle is closely tied to the previous one. When we make decisions based on impulse and emotion, we often end up making the wrong decision. When emotions guide your actions, they prevent you from seeing the potential risks in a situation or the long-term benefits. By living rationally, we live in accordance with the laws of nature. Human beings are rational beings. We are capable of choosing between what is right and wrong. By letting our behavior be controlled by our emotions, we liken ourselves to animals, which are controlled by their instincts. This principle is well captured in the words of Epictetus:

"For what is Man? A rational animal, subject to death. At once we ask, from what does the rational element distinguish us? From wild beasts. And from what else? From sheep and the like. Look to it then that you do nothing like a wild beast, else you destroy the Man in you and fail to fulfill his promise. See that you do not act like a sheep, or else again the Man in you perishes.

You ask how we act like sheep? When we consult the belly, or our passions, when our actions are random or dirty or inconsiderate, are we not falling away to the state of sheep? What do we destroy? The faculty of reason. When our actions are combative, mischievous, angry, and rude, do we not fall away and become wild beasts?

When we live a rational life, it becomes easier to fulfill our grand purpose in life. This is because we can rationally make decisions that take us closer to our goals.

Practice Non-Attachment

When Epictetus was a slave, he understood that the only thing he owned was his mind. Everything else, including his body, was not his. Instead, everything belonged to his master. By acknowledging this, Epictetus was able to live a life of happiness even though he was enslaved. We need to borrow this kind of thinking from Epictetus. This Stoic principle reminds us that we own nothing in this life. Everything can be taken away. Everything we think we own belongs to fortune. Your mansion, your cars, your beautiful wife, even the clothes you are wearing can be taken away from you. Even your healthy body can be taken away by illness. If your happiness is anchored on these things, you will be devastated when they are taken away from you.

To prevent disappointment in the event that your material possessions are taken away from you, Stoicism urges us to practice non-attachment to such objects. This does not mean that you should not work hard for material things. If you love fancy cars, buy yourself one by all means and enjoy it while you have it. However, don't get too attached to it. Fortune gives and takes, so if something is taken away from you, don't get worked up. Instead, let it go. Trust and understand that life is offering you an opportunity for personal growth.

Throw Away Vanity

According to Stoic philosophy, things are divided into three categories: the good, the bad and the indifferent. The good things are the characteristics that allows us to live a life of virtue. These include prudence, fairness, courage and temperance. The bad things are vices that keep us from living a life of virtue. These are characteristics like indulgence, cowardice, foolishness and injustice. Anything else falls in the category of indifferent things. These include things like life and death, health and sickness, pleasure and pain, and fame and bad reputation.

What most people do not realize is that the indifferent things are vanity. They simply do not matter. You can live a good and happy life whether you have these things or not. For instance, Epictetus lived a happy and virtuous life despite being a slave. You can live a life of virtue whether you are rich or poor. You can be happy whether you are employed or not. The aim of this principle is to show that Stoic philosophy and living the good life is not a preserve of a certain class. The good life is attainable to anyone, regardless of their health, wealth, social standing or looks. These things are vanity, and you should not let them keep you from living a rational and virtuous life.

However, Stoicism also understands that some indifferent things are more valuable than others. For instance, it is better to be healthy than to be sick. That is why they categorize indifferent things as either preferred or dis-preferred. Things like good health, wealth, friendship and good social status are classified as preferred, while their opposites are classified as dis-preferred.

Avoid Living a Life of Overindulgence

"First we have to reject the life of pleasure; they make us soft and womanish; they are insistent in their demands, and what is more, require us to make insistent demands on Fortune." - Seneca

As humans, we are pleasure-seeking beings. We seek for things and experiences that give us pleasure, and avoid those that bring us pain. However, what we forget is that even too much of a good thing becomes bad. For example, did you know that *even* drinking too much water can be fatal?

Like I mentioned above, Stoicism views indulgence as a bad thing. This is because indulgence is mostly driven by emotions and greed. The emotions associated with greed and indulgence keep us from making rational decisions. For instance, a few minutes of pleasure have led to many broken homes and deadly infections. Taking the easy choice is instinctive. However, since instinct is driven by emotion, it makes us forget that our actions have consequences. Cheating in a test might seem like an easy thing to do, but when you get caught, you will be expelled from school. Is it really worth it?

This principle is especially important in today's world where everything is available to us at the press of a button. A swipe on Tinder can get you an instant date, so why bother building relationships? You can get on your phone and order a meal, so why bother cooking your own? All these things seem beneficial at the moment, but on the long term, they are destructive to our personalities and lifestyles.

Stoic philosophy urges us to resist the temptation of taking the path of least resistance. Taking the easy option robs us of the opportunity to improve ourselves. Despite appearing to be so appealing, it is wrought with pitfalls and has little rewards. As a student of Stoicism, do not fall for this temptation. Avoid taking the path of least resistance.

Love Everything That Happens

"Seek not for events to happen as you wish but rather wish for events to happen as they do and your life will go smoothly." - Epictetus

This is a great quote that you should live by if you want to live a life free of disappointments. I mentioned earlier that there are things that are outside our control. When something unwanted happens to you, you have two options: you can either live in denial or accept that it has happened, learn from it and move on. Living in denial robs you of your happiness since you have no way of changing what happened. On the other hand, by accepting it and moving on, you let go of the stress from the event by acknowledging that it is not within your power to change it. The best way to let go of such things it to understand that everything happens for our greater good, even if it doesn't seem so at the moment.

This was an introductory overview of the main ideas of Stoic philosophy.

Since Stoicism needs to be applied in your daily life for it to work, each chapter contains action steps. If you apply these consistently, you *will* see the magic effects of Stoicism in your own life!

Actions Steps

- Whenever you come across a situation that threatens to rattle your emotions, ask yourself one question, "Is it within my control or not?" If it is not within your control, your default reaction should be, "It's none of my concern."
- When you experience an emotion, do not look at external causes. Instead, look inside yourself and change your reaction to whatever event triggered the emotion.
- Every day when you get up, live life like it's your last day. Remind yourself that you have limited time and make the most of it.
- Envision the worst-case scenario if you are afraid of trying something new. This will show you that you can survive even if you fail, thus giving you the confidence to overcome your fear of failure.
- You should always be present and focused in the present moment instead of focusing on the past or future.

- Do not let your decisions be based on instincts. Instead, you should take a step back and make your decisions based on rationality. When in a difficult situation, determine the right thing to do in that situation and do it regardless of the reaction of others. Focus on what you can control (your actions) and accept what you cannot control (people's reactions).
- Avoid getting too attached to material things.
- Examine different things within your life and determine where they fall. If they are good things (virtues), maintain them. If they are bad (follies), strive to eliminate them from your life. If they are indifferent, understand that they don't really matter. While you should seek preferred indifferent things, you should not let them prevent you from living a life of virtue and rationality. For instance, if you have to choose between being fair or lying in order to support your friend when they are wrong, you should opt for fairness.

- Avoid the temptation to follow the path of least resistance. Instead, face your challenges, overcome them and grow.
- When something bad happens, remind yourself that you cannot change it. Instead, accept that it has happened and trust that it is for your greater good.

In the next chapter, you are going to learn about the views of Stoic philosophy in regards to emotions and passions.

Chapter Three: Stoicism and Emotions

In this chapter, you are going to learn the views of Stoic philosophy in regards to emotions and passions.

One of the most common misconceptions about Stoicism is that the philosophy calls for people to be devoid of emotions. Most people who have heard of Stoicism believe that it encourages people to repress their passions. However, nothing could be further from the truth.

If you read through various Stoic manuals, you might come across the calls for students of Stoicism to reject emotions. However, ancient Stoics used the term emotion to refer to passions, which are *excessive* emotions. Actually, one of the central themes of Stoicism is *apatheia*, which can be taken to mean 'freedom from passions'. Stoicism advocates for us to treat excessive emotions like the weather. If you have to get to work, you will still get there whether it rains or not. The weather does not affect your ability to get to work. Similarly, we should not let emotions affect our ability to make rational decisions.

If you look at the Stoic definition of emotion, you will realize that Stoicism does not ask us to refrain from feeling or showing emotions towards people who are close to us. It does not mean that we should strive to suppress natural reactions. Instead, Stoicism divides emotions into two categories: healthy and unhealthy emotions. Healthy emotions are things like caution, delight and wishing. On the other hand, unhealthy emotions are things like fear, lust, pain and pleasure.

Remember, Stoicism urges us to focus on things that are under our control and let go of those that we cannot control. In this respect, Stoic philosophy does not call for us to suppress instinctive emotions that we cannot control. For instance, if you are faced with a life threatening situation, it is normal to feel fear, and that is okay. However, sometimes we give in to emotions that we have control over. These emotions are fueled by our wrongful perception of situations. For instance, if you are going for an interview, you might have the fear that you will fail to the extent that this fear even hinders you from performing well in your interview. This is an example of an unhealthy emotion. This fear stems from your false perception of a situation. There's nothing to show that you will actually fail. Therefore, in this case, your fear is uncalled for. It is within your control, and you can avoid it by being confident in the fact that you have prepared well for your interview.

The Stoic Meaning of Passion

When Stoic philosophy talks about passions, it refers to things that keep us from acting with rationality. These include excessive emotions that cloud our judgment as well as false opinions or perceptions of situations. Excessive emotions are those emotions that push us to do things that we would not do under normal circumstances. For instance, the quest for revenge is an excessive emotion. How many times have you heard of cases where an irate spouse kills their partner and then follows by committing suicide? In such cases, the spouse is usually angered by something the partner has done. For instance, the spouse might suspect the partner of infidelity. Sometimes, there's no actual instance of infidelity, but the main thing here is that there is a (false) perception. This results in excessive emotions (anger and the quest for revenge) that lead to the irate spouse killing their partner. Once the crime is done, the angered spouse then realizes the gravity of their actions, which is why many follow by committing suicide in order to avoid facing the consequences of their actions. In this instance, the excessive emotions cloud a person's judgment and prevent them from making rational decisions.

Luckily, most passions are temporary in nature. At the very start, they are very strong. This is the point where they might propel us to make irrational decisions. However, if they are given some time, they start to weaken, giving way to rationality. This is why it is important to avoid making decisions or acting in the heat of the moment. If you feel a strong emotion compelling you to do something, the right thing is to walk off and give yourself some time. This allows the excessive emotion to cool down and allows you to think through the situation rationally.

Finally, Stoic philosophy understands that most passions are driven by two things; fear and appetite. If we go back to our illustration about the job interview, the excessive emotion comes from the fear of not qualifying and what might follow thereafter. In our illustration about a spouse killing their partner because of some perception of wrongdoing, the excessive emotion and subsequent irrational actions are driven by the appetite for revenge.

From the Stoic definition of passion, we realize that passions are not good for us. When we are consumed by passions, they cloud our judgment and prevent us from living a life of virtue. They keep us from looking at the long-term consequences of our actions. This is why Stoic philosophy encourages its followers to suppress their passions, since giving in to passions is in contrast with one of the central objectives of Stoicism, which is to live a life of virtue and rationality.

This chapter shows that the goal of Stoicism is to have a life of joy and tranquility by avoiding excesses. Instead of being driven by our fears and appetites, we should always strive to conquer these excessive emotions. All our actions and decisions should be driven by careful deliberation.

Therefore, by asking its students to reject emotion, Stoicism does not mean that we should not care about a thing. Our ability to lead good lives depends on our ability to stop ourselves from becoming slaves to our passions.

Action Steps

- When you experience a passion, do not react right away. By reacting immediately, you do not give yourself time to contemplate your actions. You are giving in to your passions, which might cause you to make the wrong decision. Instead, take a deep breath and allow yourself to calm down.

- Seek divine guidance. Anytime you feel overburdened by an excessive emotion, close your eyes and visualize a positive solution to whatever situation you are facing. Reach out to a higher force/the universe and ask for guidance on the best way forward.

- Now that you have calmed down, find a healthy outlet for the excessive emotion. The worst thing you can do is to bottle up excessive emotions. Talk to a friend and tell them what happened. Write down what you went through in your diary. Try meditation, or any other activity that helps you release any pent-up emotions.

- Look at the bigger picture. Whatever happens to you – whether you think it is good or bad – happens for your greater good. Being able to look at an event with the understanding that it serves a higher purpose makes it easier to deal with difficult situations.

- Replace your negative thoughts with positive, affirmative thoughts. Remember, events do not affect us. Instead, we are affected by our reaction to events. Therefore, if you feel bad because of something, force out the negative thoughts and replace them with positive thoughts. Imagine yourself successfully overcoming the problem you are going through, reminisce an event that makes you smile or think about a person that makes you happy.
- Finally, forgive the triggers of your passions. This could be yourself, your spouse, your friend, and so on. When you find yourself feeling angry because of something you or someone else has done, just forgive them. By forgiving the triggers of your passions, you detach from the passions, which makes it easier for you to overcome them.

In the next chapter, you are going to learn how Stoic affirmations can help you instill a sense of control in your life and keep you from worrying about indifferent things.

Chapter Four: Affirmations for Stoicism

Affirmations are short, positive statements that you think, read or say to yourself regularly in order to help you gain confidence and achieve your goals. The use of affirmations stems from the belief that your thoughts affect your life. In this case, affirmations help you to channel your thoughts in the right direction.

By regularly repeating your affirmations, you remind yourself that it is within your power to achieve your goals or to overcome certain challenges. Affirmations help you to change your assumptions and beliefs about yourself and your perception of the things and situations around you. By repeating the affirmations to yourself, you train your subconscious mind to start believing in the affirmation.

Focus of Stoic Affirmations

Affirmations are a great tool that you can use to enhance your practice of Stoicism. However, Stoic affirmations do not focus on improving your confidence in your ability to achieve your goals. Instead, the focus of Stoic affirmations is to remind you that you should stop worrying about things outside your control, things that do not matter.

Easily Accessible and Memorable

Since affirmations are meant to be repeated regularly throughout the course of the day, they should be easily accessible and memorable. You can make your affirmations accessible by writing them down on a piece of paper and placing it in your purse or wallet. This way, you can access them and repeat them to yourself at any time of the day, whenever you need to. Alternatively, you can place your affirmations in places where you will easily see them throughout the day, such as on your desk, next to the fridge or in your bedroom. If you have the affirmations on a piece of paper in your wallet, make sure to get them out after every two hours and repeat them out loud to yourself. Similarly, when you come across the affirmations you have placed around your house, read them out loud.

Strong Belief

In addition to repeating your affirmations after every short while, you should have a strong belief in them. Using affirmations if you do not believe in them is setting yourself up for failure. This is because you will create doubts within your subconscious mind, thereby robbing the affirmations of their power. Therefore, you should only use, as affirmations, statements that you believe in. This means that if you come across a Stoic principle that you do not understand or agree with, you should not use it as an affirmation.

Examples of Stoic Affirmations

Below are some examples of Stoic affirmations that you can use. Keep in mind that these are merely examples.

You can come up with your own as you continue learning the different teachings of Stoicism. Remember, the most important thing is that you should only use affirmations that you believe in.

- *"I have no control over external circumstances."*
- *"Nothing can cause me distress without my permission."*
- *"Things don't always have to go my way."*
- *"My happiness depends not on external conditions. Instead, it comes from within."*
- *"I am in control of my emotions, not the other way round."*
- *"I should always live a life of virtue and rationality."*
- *"It makes no sense arguing with the will of nature."*

Goal of Stoic affirmations

The aim of Stoic affirmations is to prevent you from becoming a slave to your emotions. For instance, when things do not go your way, you can use such affirmations to remind yourself that there is no need to sweat it out since it was not within your control. When you experience negative emotions, you can repeat the *"Nothing can cause me distress without my permission"* affirmation to remind yourself that the negative emotion is actually a result of your perception of the situation. By changing your perception, you can get rid of the negative emotion. In case you find yourself in a distressing situation, read out your affirmations aloud and remind yourself that there is no cause for anxiety.

Most of the above affirmations are meant to show you that you have no control over the world. The underlying message is that you can live a virtuous and happy life regardless of external situations.

Action Steps

- Develop your own affirmations and keep them in an easily accessible place where you can reach them whenever you need them.
- Set affirmation traps for yourself within your home and workplace and repeat the affirmation whenever you come across them.

In the next chapter, you are going to learn about Stoic practices that you can use to make yourself an oasis of calmness amidst the chaos that defines modern society.

Chapter Five: Stoic Practices to Help You Retain Your Calmness In the Madness of Modern Society

In this chapter, you are going to learn how to maintain control over your life in the madness of modern day society.

Today's society is very chaotic. We have multiple demands on our time, from our jobs to our friends and family. We want to be accepted and liked by others. Moreover, there is always something vying for our attention. In every little decision, from what we eat for breakfast to what we should watch on TV or what we should buy our partners for their birthday, we are presented with dozens of options to choose from. There are simply too many distractions. Everyone is trying to influence us, from advertisers to our colleagues at work to our friends.

This can make us feel like we are losing control of our lives. How do you regain control? How do you thrive in this madness that has become the definition of modern society? Below are some Stoic practices that you can use to get your life back on track and instill a sense of calmness in the midst of chaos.

Become an Internal Oasis Of Control

Many of the things that make us lose our minds are things that we have no control over. Therefore, it doesn't make a lot of sense to fret over them. It doesn't matter how angry we get at them, there is nothing we can do to change them. Therefore, getting worked up because of such things is a quick recipe for duress and distress in our lives. This is especially true in today's modern society where we are so used to comforts that we treat every slight inconvenience like the end of the world. Remember, our emotions do not stem from things happening to us, but rather from our perception of the events and our reactions to them. By altering our reactions to external events, we can remain calm and in control regardless of what happens.

To illustrate this point, let's look at the life of Epictetus, who was taken into slavery. It would seem that Epictetus had no control over anything. His master was in charge of *everything*. However, to Epictetus, this did not affect him. He realized he had control over his mind and soul. No one could take that away from him. He was able to lead a purposeful life despite being a slave who had nothing to his name.

Think about that for a moment...

Can you imagine what it's like being a slave?

Surely, this must be one of the hardest way to live, even if your master treats you relative well. It doesn't require much effort to understand that such a life must be very depressing. Yet, even in these difficult

circumstances, Epictetus was able to live purposefully.
A true inspiration!

Like Epictetus, we should always maintain control over
our opinions, judgments, perceptions and desires.
Instead of letting these external events get us worked
up, we can create an oasis of calmness around
ourselves by choosing to focus on what we can control,
which is our emotions. We can maintain our happiness
regardless of what is happening around us.

Remain in Charge Of Your Own Happiness

Human beings are social creatures. This means that we
have an innate need to be part of a social group, the
need to be accepted by others. However, sometimes we
let this need for acceptance dictate a large part of our
lives to the extent that we peg our happiness and self-
esteem on others. We live our lives trying to get others
to accept us. We think that we will be happy once
others perceive us in certain way. This need for

acceptance starts influencing our choices, our actions and our decisions. Everything is done to please others. What we forget is that we have no control over other people's views of us. Therefore, if we peg our happiness on other people's acceptance of us, we will never truly be happy. In the words of the popular saying, if you live for people's acceptance, you will die from their rejection.

As a student of Stoicism, you should learn to let go of this need for acceptance. This is because this need for acceptance deprives you of the freedom of living your life on your own terms. Instead of making decisions and taking actions that are best for you, you do things that you think others will approve of, even if they are detrimental to your happiness and well-being. This need for acceptance keeps you from achieving your true potential. Instead, it keeps you stuck in a state of anxiety and worry.

To let go of this need, you should examine your actions and decisions and try to understand whether they are right or whether they stem from the need for approval by others. If you find yourself in a situation where you want to make a decision that doesn't feel right to you, pause and consider why you are making it. If it is out of the fear of what others will think about you, reconsider what the right choice for you is and go with it. Finally, you should learn to believe in yourself, because the excessive need for approval is usually a result of low self-confidence. No one is perfect, and therefore you should not live a life of enslavement trying to please others.

Maintain Your Focus in The Face Of Distractions

The modern world we live in today is full of distractions. At any one moment, there are a dozen things vying for our attention. There are lots of temptations and our minds are full of thoughts, anxiety and worry. All these things keep us distracted from our goals and objectives. For us to achieve our goals, we need to remain focused and eliminate all these temptations and distractions from our minds.

As a student of Stoicism, you should be ready to live a life full of purpose. Rather than simply reacting to things as they happen, regain control over your life by living intentionally. To do this, you need to have a clear idea of your purpose and goals. The following quote by Seneca illustrates this well: *"If a person doesn't know to which port they sail, no wind is favorable."*

In his book *Life on Purpose*, Victor J. Strecher, Ph.D., Professor of Health Behavior & Health Education at the University of Michigan, writes:

"I felt that finding my purpose was like a boat finding the right current and wind that then moves me effortlessly at a high speed. My only "job"—purposeful living—is to find this current and wind and to be able to steer within them."

To find your purpose, Strecher suggests writing down:

- Your core values
- What matters most to you in your life
- Assembling your core values and goals into an overall life purpose. This doesn't have to be one single purpose. It's perfectly fine to break it up into different parts, such as family, work and community.

To keep your goals clear in your mind, it also helps to create a vision board, in order to stay focused on your goals. When faced with distractions, looking at your vision board will remind you what you need to do to achieve your goals, thereby making it easier for you to get rid of distractions. Many of our distractions also come in the form of anxiety and worry. Stoicism teaches us to let go of things that we cannot control and to live our lives free of fear or appetite. If something is not within your control, don't let it distract your focus. Similarly, do not let the fear of the future worry you to the extent that you lose focus of the now.

Remember That Nothing Lasts Forever

A lot of the distress we experience today stems from the anxiety of trying to be seen as achievers. However, we should remember that, in the end, our achievements do not really matter. In Chapter Two, I said that we should live every day like our last. If today was your last day on earth, would you really be bothered by material things? Would you care about your job title, the kind of car you drive or your home address? Probably not.

In his letters, Seneca spoke extensively about meditating on death. Also, Epictetus taught that when kissing a loved one, his students should remind themselves that they are mortal. In Medieval times, Christian monks would greet each other saying *"Memento Mori"*, which translates as *"Remember that you will die."*

We should strive to free our minds of the worry and anxiety of seeking to be seen as important. You might work hard and become the richest person in the world, but the moment you die, another person will take your place and your name will only be reduced to an entry in history books. And that's only if you accomplished something noteworthy! Similarly, all the achievements you are chasing after won't last. The moment that you realize that all these pressures and expectations are insignificant is the moment that you will learn to live a life of freedom. Do not sacrifice your life and happiness in exchange for material gain.

Be Assertive

In today's society, temptations are everywhere. Every now and then, your friends and colleagues will try to influence you to do things that go against your better judgment. Your boss might try to coerce and intimidate you into doing something that does not feel right. In all these situations, you need to stand your ground and overcome these temptations and influences, guided by your moral compass. Remember, the goal of Stoicism is to live a life of virtue. Do not let greed or fear compromise your virtues. Instead, you should always be steadfast in what you believe in and stand your ground.

Action Steps

- Learn to control your perceptions, opinions and judgments of things happening around you. This will help you to develop an internal oasis of control in a world of chaos.
- Learn how to live a life that is independent of the opinion of others. Do things not because of what others will think about you, but rather because they are right.
- Regain control by living your life intentionally, rather than by simply reacting to things as they happen.
- Remind yourself each day that nothing lasts forever. Do not obsess over achievements and titles because they won't last forever. Instead, aspire to live a good life free from irrational pressures and expectations.

- Determine what is good and bad by your moral compass and be steadfast in your belief. Do not let people coerce, shame, intimidate or in any other way influence you to do something that you don't believe is right.

In the next chapter, you are going to learn some steps you can follow to incorporate Stoic philosophy into your daily life.

Chapter Six: Implementing Stoicism in Your Daily Life

In this chapter, you are going to learn some step-by-step guidelines you can follow to implement Stoicism in your day-to-day life.

Stoicism is an active philosophy, which means that it is not enough to simply read about its principles. Instead, you also need to put the teachings of Stoic philosophy into practice in your daily life. So, how do you incorporate and implement Stoicism into your daily life? Below are some tips on how you can practice the Stoic philosophy.

Meditate Every Morning

Stoicism is a philosophy that involves a lot of self-reflection. To become a true student of Stoicism, you must learn the art of self-reflection. A good way of doing this is to get into the habit of meditating every morning before you start your day. Every morning, make it a habit to read one quote from the ancient Stoic philosophers and meditate on it. Try to understand its inner meaning and find ways in which the teachings of this quote can be applied in your day to day life. By doing so, you will move from being a passive student to an active one who puts into practice what they learn. This will also give you the motivation to continue practicing Stoic philosophy.

Practice Daily Ethical Mindfulness

I have talked about mindfulness a number of times so far. This is because practicing awareness is a very important part of Stoic philosophy. Every day, at every moment, you should pay attention to what is happening in the present. Mindfulness is about living in the here and now. To practice ethical mindfulness, you should let go of the past and the future. The past is gone, and you can do nothing to change it. No one knows the future, so you have no control over that either. It is illogical to obsess over the past and the future when they are out of your control. Instead, make the most of now, the present moment.

Maintain A Diary

Stoic philosophy places a lot of focus on living a life of reflection. Every evening, before you go to sleep, you should take a few minutes to sit quietly and review your day. Both Seneca and Marcus Aurelius were huge advocates of this kind of introspection. Actually, Marcus Aurelius' *Meditations* was written in this manner. Every evening, he would reflect on his day, consider what he had done well that day, pinpoint the areas where he had made improvements and identify areas that still needed improvement.

By examining your day this way, you are able to identify situations during the day where you failed to act with virtue and come up with ways of improving yourself. When you do this, do not hide anything from yourself. If you find any shortcomings in your actions throughout the day, do not berate yourself. Instead, pardon yourself and make a commitment to ensuring that you never repeat the same mistakes.

Actively Study Stoic Philosophy

While I said that Stoicism is an active philosophy, this does not mean that you should stop trying to deepen your knowledge of Stoic principles. Commit to reading books on Stoicism every day. Not only should you read, you should also teach others about the Stoic philosophy. The best way to learn, understand and internalize something is by teaching others about it. For instance, you can find and join a local Stoic group where you can discuss Stoic philosophy with other members.

Envision Life Without Things You Enjoy Today

There is a common saying that we only miss the waters when the well runs dry. No one understood this saying better than the ancient Stoics. According to Stoic philosophy, by acknowledging that the things we enjoy today might not be available forever, we become more appreciative of them. What better way of reminding yourself this than deliberately denying yourself these things temporarily? By waiting for the bus on your way to work one morning, you become more appreciative of the convenience that comes with being able to drive to work in your own car. Similarly, by going without lunch one day, you become more appreciative of the fact that you can afford lunch on a daily basis.

Doing this reminds us that the things we take for granted are actually important. It makes us aware of the small miracles in our lives that we ignore each day. It also shows us that even if some of the good things we have in life are taken away, it does not mean the end of the world for us. This makes us more resilient and helps us to develop self-discipline.

Always Remember That Time Is Your Most Valuable Resource

"No man can escape his destiny, the net inquiry being how best he may live the time that he has to live." - Marcus Aurelius

One of the key pillars of Stoic philosophy is the understanding and acknowledgement of our mortality. You should understand that time is the only non-renewable resource given to you. Knowing that your time on earth is limited is a very sobering thought that should make you humble while at the same time push you to achieve the best you can.

Tim Urban's popular blog post *'The Tail End'* on the 'WaitButWhy' blog illustrates this wonderfully, by laying out the human lifespan visually. I have multiple friends who, after reading this article, realized how little parent time they had left, and set the intention to spend more quality time with them.

When they are at old age or even on their deathbeds, most people do not regret any of the things they did. Instead, they regret the things they did not do, the chances they did not take.

A friend of mine told me that his 82-year-old aunt regrets not dancing enough when she was young and fit. Now it's too late: she doesn't have the fitness and endurance to dance the way should want to.

Knowing that you have limited time in the world should spur you to make the most of today. Similarly, when you find yourself in a tough situation, you should remind yourself that it will not last forever.

Whenever you hesitate to do something, because it's scary, or perhaps frowned upon by others, ask yourself: will I regret *not* doing this when I'm old? If the answer is yes, then go ahead and do it! As Gary Vaynerchuk has emphasized many times, regret is the scariest thing in the world.

Reflect on What You Spend The Most Time On

"It is not that we have short space of time, but that we waste much of it." - Seneca

This point is closely linked to the previous one. Time is the most precious and the only non-renewable resource that we are given in life. Unfortunately, like Seneca observes in his quote above, most of us do not place much value on our time. We end up wasting a lot of time doing things that do not really matter. As a student of Stoicism, you should make it a habit to reflect on the things that you spend most of your time on and determine whether they are moving you closer to your goals and objectives.

Before you can determine whether the things you spend time on are moving you closer to your goals, you need to have a clear definition of what you want to achieve in life. If you do not know where you are going, any road will take you there. Only by knowing what you want can you then focus on the right things and avoid wasting time on things that do not really matter. One way to identify what you spend the most time on is to practice the ritual of evening reflection. Every evening, while writing your evening diary, give some thought to the things you spent your time doing during the day. Are they in alignment with your goals? If you find yourself spending huge chunks of your day on things that do not move you closer to your goals, find a way of eliminating these things from your day. A good way of eliminating them from your day is having a morning ritual where you make plans for your day. When you are aware of what you should be doing throughout the day, you are less likely to waste your time on unproductive activities.

Avoid Getting Sucked into The Cycle Of Materialism

One of the gravest mistakes you can make that will rob happiness from your life is to fall into the cycle of materialism. At the same time, this is something that has become very common today. Many people think that the secret to happiness in life is having more money and more stuff. As a student of Stoicism, you should realize that money is an indifferent thing. It does not affect your ability to live a life of virtue and happiness. How many people are remembered because of the money or stuff they had? Virtually none. Instead, people are remembered for their accomplishments and their contributions towards the advancement of the world.

Therefore, you should not let yourself become caught up in this cycle, since it will only make you miserable. This is why you see billionaires who are unhappy with their lives. They chase money only to realize later that it has no value in their lives. Some even feel the need to redeem themselves, such as industrialist and millionaire Henry Clay Frick. At one point, Frick was known as the most hated man in America, after hiring mercenaries to end the 1892 Homestead Plant strike. Concerned about his legacy, he declared in his will that his house, which included a large and valuable art collection, was to become a museum. It is now considered one of the most extraordinary private art collections in the world.

To break free of this cycle of getting stuck in materialism, you should stop associating happiness to material things. Don't let your decisions be influenced by societal expectations. Stop comparing your life to your friends and neighbors or trying to keep up with them. Learn to identify the important things in your life that are not tied to materialism.

Be Cheerful in All Your Interactions

According to Stoic philosophy, we have within us everything we need for our happiness. Happiness is not dependent on external factors. Instead, it comes from within and from appreciating whatever is around us. Therefore, as a student of Stoic philosophy, we should always be cheerful. To do this, we should learn to control our reactions to external events to ensure that they do not bring us distress. If someone cuts you off in traffic, you can choose to get angry and insult them, or you can choose to let it go and give them the right of way. By choosing to let go, their actions do not affect your happiness. Another way to remain cheerful is to live with the knowledge that things will not always go our way. Once you acknowledge this, you will remain cheerful even when things do not work out as you wanted.

Power Lies Not in Knowledge, But In What You Do With It

"Don't just say you have read books. Show that through them you have learned to think better, to be a more discriminating and reflective person. Books are the training weights of the mind. They are very helpful, but it would be a bad mistake to suppose that one has made progress simply by having internalized their contents." - Epictetus

Finally, you need to realize that simply having knowledge is not enough. You need to apply that knowledge. As Epictetus says in the above quote, you make no progress by internalizing the contents of books. True power comes from what you decide to do with the knowledge. You must commit yourself to putting into practice all the knowledge you learn from Stoic philosophy.

Action Steps

- Meditate on a classical Stoicism quote every morning, reading it several times and reflecting on what it means.
- Learn to pay attention to the present by practicing ethical mindfulness. Free your mind of worries about the past and the future.
- Every evening, reflect on the events of the day that just ended and write your thoughts in a diary. Find out what you did wrong and how you can make the next day better.
- Aspire to learn something new about Stoic philosophy each day and internalize the knowledge by teaching others.

- Practice misfortune to learn how to be appreciative of the little things in life and to teach yourself how to cope if they are taken away by any chance.
- Learn to appreciate time as your most precious resource and live your life to the fullest, knowing well that your time here is limited.
- Reflect on what you spend the most time on. This will help you to focus your thoughts and actions on things that are aligned with your goals in life.
- Avoid falling into the cycle of materialism. Reign in your desires and you will enjoy greater satisfaction from what you already have.
- Always be cheerful in all your interactions. Seek happiness, not from indifferent things, but from spreading goodness to the world.
- Commit yourself to putting into practice the principles of Stoic philosophy. Power comes not from knowledge, but from what we choose to do with the knowledge.

Final Words

One night, while recording his thoughts for what would later be known as his *Meditations*, Marcus Aurelius wrote:

"Your principles can't be extinguished unless you snuff out the thoughts that feed them, for it's continually in your power to reignite new ones...It's possible to start living again! See things anew as you once did – that is how to restart life!"

I want to thank you for making it all the way to the end of this book. You know have a basic understanding of what Stoicism is.

You:

- now know where Stoicism originated and what its key principles and beliefs are.

- have learned the view of Stoicism towards emotions and passions and how you can use Stoic affirmations to regain your control during times of distress.
- have also learned a number of Stoic practices that will help you thrive in the madness of modern society, as well as a step-by-step guideline of steps you can follow to implement Stoicism in your daily life.

With this knowledge, you are now ready to, as Marcus Aurelius put it, "*start living again!*"

How?

By putting the tools and practices you learned to use. Remember, Stoicism is an *active* philosophy. It is not enough to simply accept the value of Stoicism intellectually. In the same you can't know what coffee tastes like by merely reading about it, Stoicism too needs to be experienced through your actions in day-to-day life.

This book only scratched the surface of what Stoicism is all about. If you would like to continue learning about the Stoics, and how you can become one yourself, I suggest you pick up one of the books I recommend in the 'Resources' section.

Good luck as you embark on your journey of transformation!

Resources

Classical books on Stoicism

- *Discourses and Selected Writings* – Epictetus
- *The Enchiridion* – Epictetus
- *Complete Works of Seneca the Younger* – Lucius Annaeus Seneca
- *Meditations* – Marcus Aurelius

Contemporary Books on Stoicism

- *The Daily Stoic: 366 Meditations on Wisdom, Perseverance, and the Art of Living* – Ryan Holiday & Stephen Hanselman
- *The Guided Tour: Stoic Serenity: A Practical Guide to Finding Inner Peace* – Keith Seddon
- *Stoicism* – John Sellars

- *The Stoics: A Guide for the Perplexed* – Andrew Holowchak
- *A Guide to the Good Life: The Ancient Art of Stoic Joy* – William Irvine
- *The Stoics* – F. H. Sandbach
- *How to Be a Stoic: Using Ancient Philosophy to Live a Modern Life* – Massimo Pigliucci
- *A Guide to the Good Life: The Ancient Art of Stoic Joy* – William B. Irvine
- *Philosophy for Life and Other Dangerous Situations: Ancient Philosophy for Modern Problems* – Jules Evans
- *Rome's Last Citizen: The Life and Legacy of Cato, Mortal Enemy of Caesar* – Rob Goodman & Jimmy Soni
- *Courage Under Fire: Testing Epictetus's Doctrines in a Laboratory of Human Behavior (Hoover Essays)* – James B. Stockdale
- *Stoicism and the Art of Happiness (Teach Yourself: Philosophy & Religion)* – Donald Robertson
- *Stoicism and Emotion* – Margaret Graver

- *The Inner Citadel: The Meditations of Marcus Aurelius (Meditations of Marcus Aurelius)* – Pierre Hadot

Websites on Stoicism

- dailystoic.com
- modernstoicism.com
- stoicfellowship.com
- reddit.com/r/stoicism/
- philosophyforbeginners.com/philosophers/introduction-to-stoicism/
- apparentstoic.com
- immoderatestoic.com

Podcasts on Stoicism

- Stoic Meditations
- Good Fortune
- Stoic Mettle

- The Sunday Stoic
- Stoic Solutions
- The Practical Stoic
- The Tim Ferriss Show (technically, this is not a podcast only on Stoicism. However, Tim Ferriss is devout Stoic and brings it up a lot on his show)

BONUS CHAPTER: What Is Minimalism?

Below, you will find a free bonus chapter from my book '**MINIMALISM 101**: How Minimalist Living Can Help You To Declutter, Tidy Up Your Stuff and Say Goodbye to Things You Don't Need.'

It is my way of saying thanks for reading this book on Stoicism. You rock!

Let's get started, shall we?

***

In this chapter, we will define just what 'minimalism' is and see just how widely-applied this concept is.

What is Minimalism

The term minimalism applies when you reduce a subject to just its necessary elements and strip away the things that distract or don't add true value. It's a very much 'less is more' kind of concept.

Minimalism is used in art, music, literature, and architecture. In art, minimalist pieces are often based on geometric shapes, repetition, and neutral surfaces. In music, minimalism takes shape in the iteration of simple sequences of chords. In literature, the written word is used sparingly, allowing the reader to engage with the text and draw out their own meaning of the work rather than see it through the author's eyes. In architecture, arguably one of the most well-known forms of minimalism – thanks to the rise of the Japanese Zen philosophy in pop culture – is the style where a building or a room is minimized to the point where nothing more can be taken from the design to improve its look.

Seeing the pattern? Minimalism is all about letting the subject take the main stage by removing all the clutter and noise around it.

Minimalist Lifestyle

What is a minimalist lifestyle? It's when you get rid of your car, your house, live in an empty yet Zen-like white room, practice yoga every day, only eat wholesome organic food, travel to exotic yet peaceful destinations, and live with just a small suitcase of possessions.

I'm kidding! It's not like that at all.

However, some people are wary of a minimalist life as they feel it has all of these restrictions. They promptly decide that this is not for them as they couldn't possibly live without these things. Many people wrongly connect a minimalist lifestyle to a hippie way of living. They associate it to meditation and emptying your home of all its belongings. If that's what you want

– to meditate, to clear your home out, to live as a hippie – that's great! If it makes you feel good and minimalism can help you do that, of course.

However, if you think that minimalism is just that, you're missing its real meaning.

Minimalism can be applied anywhere – from the financial broker, to the freelancer, to the stay-at-home mom or dad – and isn't just for those with loads of free time to enter a Zen-like state on a regular basis. In fact, you don't even need to give up everything you own. The real meaning of minimalism is often distorted or exaggerated.

Minimalism doesn't frown upon having material possessions. It acknowledges that there isn't anything wrong in owning things. However, it also encourages you to think about how much value you assign to certain items. It invites you to minimize materialism, where we place so much significance on material goods that we prioritize it above other things in our life such as:

- friends and family,
- personal development
- pursuing passions
- our health, and
- contributions to society

It pushes you to think about what really matters and get rid of the stuff that doesn't.

If having a big house and a large garden is your dream and it matters to you, do it. Likewise, if traveling the world with just one suitcase is what makes you happy, then make it happen. Minimalism isn't about not spending or being extra frugal – it's about making conscious decisions about what items you want in your life that will bring value and help you achieve your goals. It's about thinking before you buy something impulsively that you don't need and can make you feel guilty after. It's about breaking out of the consumer culture, slowing down, and making purchases after careful deliberation. Minimalism helps align your values and goals with the items you have so everything around you serves a purpose, rather than being there for the sake of it.

People who follow a minimalist lifestyle don't all slot into one neat category. I follow a minimalist lifestyle and still have things such as a laptop and writing equipment. Naturally, I'm surrounded by friends and acquaintances, as we often are when we adopt a certain way of life or hobby, who also follow a minimalist lifestyle. My friend, Andrew Squires, travels regularly and can fit almost all his belongings into one large backpack, ready to embark on the next adventure. On the other hand, another friend of mine, Sofie Quinn, is excelling in her career in exports and has a house, a nice car, and still has a minimalist approach to life.

It's clear our lives are different yet we all share one common (and important) trait – we are all minimalists. How? Put simply, we have all surrounded ourselves with only the things we need or truly value by getting rid of the excess and clutter that were clouding out what really matters in our lives. We have deliberately chosen to seek out a life that is fulfilling and free, and one that is meaningful and full of purpose. Everything we have then contributes in some way to this, and ultimately to our happiness.

So, if I had to sum up minimalism in one sentence, it would be:

Minimalism is the pursuit of happiness and fulfilment through life itself by following what drives us, rather than looking for purpose and meaning in material objects.

This is how minimalism can be applied to anybody and everybody. Everyone has a different purpose in life and something that sparks their fire. Minimalism helps you find and nourish that, leading you to having a happier life that aligns your passions, your purpose, and your values.

It's not easy to adopt a minimalist lifestyle, at least not in the beginning. It requires deliberate thoughts and taking a long, hard look at what really matters to you. You need to be honest with yourself. However, it does get easier and eventually – I promise! – it becomes a mindset so ingrained that it's a part of you. Just keep taking it step by step and you will get there.

Everything in this book will help you, so don't worry about *how* to do it, as I will show you.

Action Steps

- Consider what you truly value and what is important to you. Is it having a family? Having a good job? Traveling? Buy a house? Perhaps it's all of these things.

- Take some time to deliberately think about what you value and make sure these are the things *you* want, not what you think others want for you.

- Make a list of what is important to you and what your goals are for the future. Make them as concise and detailed as possible. These may change in the future and that's fine. Right now, it's important to focus on how you are feeling and what drives you at this moment.

- These two lists are what give you your purpose. You want to be doing things that align with your values (what's important to you) and help you fulfill your purpose (your goals for the future).

- Keep these lists in an easy-to-see area so you are constantly reminded of who you are and where you want to be. This is the first step of beginning a minimalist life.

***

This is the end of this bonus chapter.

Want to continue reading?

Then get your copy of "Minimalism 101" at your favorite bookstore!

Did You Like This Book?

If you enjoyed this book, I would like to ask you for a favor. Would you be kind enough to share your thoughts and post a review of this book? Just a few sentences would already be really helpful.

Your voice is important for this book to reach as many people as possible.

The more reviews this book gets, the more people will be able to find it and also apply the Stoic principles in their life!

***

IF YOU DID NOT LIKE THIS BOOK, THEN PLEASE TELL ME! You can email me at **feedback@semsoli.com**, to share with me what you did not like.

Perhaps I can change it.

A book does not have to be stagnant, in today's world. With feedback from readers like yourself, I can improve the book. So you can impact the quality of this book, and I welcome your feedback. Help make this book better for everyone!

Thank you again for reading this book and good luck with applying everything you have learned!

I'm rooting for you...

By The Same Author

ACCELERATED LEARNING
How to Learn Fast With Ease

Kevin Garnett

DECLUTTER YOUR LIFE

The Art of Tidying Up, Organizing Your Home,
Decluttering Your Mind, & Minimalist Living
(Less is More!)

KEVIN GARNETT

MINIMALISM
101

HOW MINIMALIST LIVING CAN HELP YOU TO DECLUTTER, TIDY UP YOUR STUFF AND SAY GOODBYE TO THINGS YOU DON'T NEED.

KEVIN GARNETT

SELF
DISCIPLINE
101

Get Things Done By Learning How To Use Habits,
Routines and Mental Toughness to Achieve
Your Goals

Kevin Garnett

Notes

CPSIA information can be obtained
at www.ICGtesting.com
Printed in the USA
LVHW080857131022
730610LV00015B/1015